Dad Logic
Observations from the Fatherly Trenches

Jim Maxwell

ISBN-13: 978-1535128933
ISBN-10: 1535128933

DEDICATION

This book is dedicated to my wife Teresa and my children who begged to remain anonymous, lest I embarrass them. Consider that promise kept Michael, Patrick, Joseph, Katherine, Thomas and Anne.

CONTENTS

Preface   i

Acknowledgments   iii

A Vacation **With** the Kids is a Vacation **For** the Kids   1

As the Phones Get Smarter, The People Get Dumber   3

Who Stole My Plane Tickets?   5

Antisocial Media   7

Soap Opera Sports Coverage   9

Where is the Outrage Over the Dad Stereotype?   13

Gotcha   17

When Did Attitude Replace Composure as a Desired Attribute?   19

TV Trauma (Are You a Victim?)   21

Beware the Helicopter Parents and Treat Monitors   25

Is Everyone a Victim Now?   27

Are Magnet Schools Affecting Earth's Orbit?   31

Parent Fashion   33

Tired Young People   35

When Did Competition Become a Bad Thing?   37

Dads and Volunteering   41

The Extended Isolation Principle   43

Box Ticker Couples   47

Welcome to Judgemart   51

An Overabundance of Parenting Expertise   55

Advice for New Dads Regarding Childbirth   59

PREFACE

This book has no greater goal than to make you laugh while appreciating a dad's view of life's idiosyncrasies. While dads are mostly portrayed as incapable morons, we do have an occasional thought that ventures beyond beer and sex.

Another misnomer about fathers is that we don't have much to say. Oh, we have plenty to say, but we've been trained not to say much if we want peace at home and the workplace. We keep most of our comments to ourselves and ulcers have never had it better. I believe most dads would whole heartedly agree with many of the views expressed throughout this book. Some dads will categorically deny subscribing to said views depending on who is standing next to them or who is posing the question.

Moms have a large share of voice in the media and online. It stands to reason because, as a group, they are better communicators than dads and more eager to share information. I wrote this book because dads have so little share of voice. Our silence is often misinterpreted as agreement or complicity.

Like most dads, I've spent my adult life shrugging off the stereotypes and keeping most of my opinions under the radar. Male bashing is easy and justified in some cases. Men do stupid things that deserve criticism. However, you reach a point in your life where you want to set the record straight on some preconceived notions (while still coherent enough to do so). More importantly, you have to sit back and laugh at it all or else you'll lose your mind.

As a father of six children, I write from experience rather than theory. I have a wonderful wife who will probably go into hiding after this book is published. I thoroughly enjoy watching my children develop their own unique personalities while sharing many of the same strengths and flaws passed down from mom and dad.

Jim Maxwell

ACKNOWLEDGMENTS

I would like to thank my mother (Mary) for teaching me how to laugh at life, and my late father (Chuck) who was totally devoted to his children and grandchildren.

I have no one to thank regarding this book because I didn't ask anyone if it was a good idea. I already knew the answer but wrote it anyway. If you would like to blame someone, blame everyone who ever laughed at me. Both were heavily medicated at the time, but they still count.

A VACATION **WITH** THE KIDS IS A VACATION **FOR** THE KIDS

As the departure date neared for any of our family road trips, coworkers and friends would ask where "I" was taking a vacation. I paused because I would never refer to one of our family road trips as a vacation for me or my wife. When we returned, people would ask me if I enjoyed the vacation. Again, I would pause before answering because if I told them the truth, they would never have children or take their existing children beyond the driveway. My standard response would be, "Fine." If they persisted in search of more detail, I would calmly respond, "A vacation **with** the children is a vacation **for** the children."

Air-traffic controller is reportedly one of the most stressful jobs. I contend that driving a van across the country with two teenagers, two tweens and two toddlers comes awfully close.

The time-honored road trip with a large family is a much different experience than a family with say one or two kids. Let me explain.

Families with one or two kids will plan their entire route and carefully time any stops around the kids' sleeping schedules. Larger families will do the same, but the trip will

1

quickly dissolve into making it from one rest stop to the next without killing each other.

Families with one or two kids will eat wherever they please. Larger families will eat out of coolers or at an all-you-can-eat buffet, where the parents sit in a separate booth and pretend the loud kids in the booth next to them are not their own.

Parents of one or two kids will whisper so as not to wake the sleeping children in the back seat. Parents of larger families will scream over the heads of sleeping infants to scold the older kids. By the way, that is why the younger kids are always better dorm room sleepers.

Parents of one or two kids panic when a child starts crying in the back seat. Parents of larger families panic when no noise is coming from the back seat.

As road trips approached, people would ask me what movies the kids were going to watch in the van. They would recoil in horror when I said there would be no movies. Yes, my wife and I had the audacity to expect our children to entertain themselves via unorthodox methods such as books, games and actual conversation. That may sound like I'm preaching but let's be honest; can you remember the last time you could get eight people to agree on what to watch? Why argue about that when we already have so much to argue about?

One final note - Tourist attractions that place gift shops at every exit, with toys displayed at a toddler's eye level, deserve a special place in hell. I understand product placement but that practice unabashedly throws every parent under the bus. It's like exiting a weight loss center through a donut shop.

AS THE PHONES GET SMARTER, THE PEOPLE GET DUMBER

I love technology. However, if you are the father of a large family, you can't afford to keep up with some of the higher-end gadgets. Those of us who grew up without today's technology have always understood the difference between "want" and "need" when it comes to the latest and greatest.

I find my smart phone extremely useful, but if you take it away, I'll survive. Take a smart phone from a teen or millennial and they'll implode within an hour. Some parents will do the same. Technology is here to stay, and I'm perfectly fine with that. However, poor phone etiquette has reached epidemic proportions, and it deserves further examination.

Mobile phone etiquette among some teens and adults is atrocious. You greet them, and some don't even look up from their phone. When you try to address them, they either ignore you or flash that look of annoyance because you dared to pull them away from that all-important photo of their best friend's cousin's brother eating the best taco EVER. My personal favorite is when they pull out the phone and start dialing or texting while you're talking to them.

Can you imagine the train wrecks that will occur when

some of these teens attend their first, real job interview? I don't wish them ill, but part of me wants to bring some popcorn and sit in on that first interview.

As I said, it's not all on the kids. Poor phone etiquette is practiced by many who are old enough to know better.

My favorites are the people who share the most intimate details of their love life or latest medical condition with everyone on the elevator, on the plane, in the theater and in the waiting room. I've walked away from waiting rooms knowing more about a stranger's prostate exam than my own. I can't get my son to tell me the name of the girl he is taking to prom, but I know that the lady (Cindy), who stood behind me at the DMV, has a boyfriend named Conner. Conner is upset over Cindy's "infection," and Conner never lifts the toilet seat.

One final note – People at the front of food ordering lines, who make the rest of us wait while they chat on their phones, should be ordered to lie face down on the floor while the rest of us walk over them to place our orders.

WHO STOLE MY PLANE TICKETS?

My father was a very organized man. He was a meticulous planner, and nothing irritated him more than when things didn't go as planned. His job required regular travel, and his plane tickets always seemed to vanish the morning of his departure. After a failed search for the tickets, exasperation would take over, and he would address no one in particular by loudly asking, "WHO STOLE MY PLANE TICKETS?" My siblings and I always got a good laugh out of that one. We still say it out loud when we can't find something.

I am not as organized as my father. Dads know where the important stuff is as long as no one moves it without our knowledge. The second part of the previous sentence is critical to this observation. Few things are as frustrating to a dad than reaching for the one item he desperately needs, and it's gone because someone decided it belonged elsewhere or wasn't important enough to keep.

Yes, men are pack rats, and we certainly contribute to the clutter. However, if you take inventory of the household clutter, I think you'll find that the fatherly contribution is no larger than any other household member. It just looks larger because it's often unorganized.

My wife disguises her clutter by organizing it and storing it in every available storage space. On the rare occasion some space opens up, she fills it faster than an empty parking space in Manhattan. Her initiative wins the day because my clutter has no place to go but everywhere else. And when your clutter is everywhere, your clutter becomes expendable junk.

Once my wife deems something of mine obsolete or worthy of disposal, she will either throw said items away or let me know I need to do something with them by lining them up on my side of the bed. I admire the simplicity of the bed dump maneuver. However, it's about as subtle as a professional wrestler taking a chair to the head.

I know what some of you are thinking and yes, I tried to turn the tables once, but only once. I placed some of her little-used items on her side of the bed and that did not end well. She returned the items to their rightful place, and there was an icy chill in our house for a few days. That instance erased any confusion I may have had on the topic. I learned that her clutter would never drop down to the level of my expendable junk. And most of my clutter probably is junk. Its actual value is nonexistent. Its sentimental value is priceless if you value random pop culture icons and references… as most men do.

One final note – Our household clutter approaches mythical status as our older kids near the age of moving out. We use their future living space needs to justify holding on to everything. A common quote in our household is, "Don't throw that away. The kids may need it." That sounds reasonable until one day your basement looks like a pawn shop, or you find yourself watching a rerun of *Hoarders,* and the featured home seems just fine to you.

ANTISOCIAL MEDIA

Despite the chapter title, I don't hate social media. I'm just calling it as I see it. I remain surprised at how social media entities and users claim that social media makes people more "social." Dads are often ridiculed for their lack of social media prowess but there are good reasons for the avoidance.

I don't blame the providers. Who knew that humanity would take technology intended to enhance communication and turn it into a fire hose for uninformed opinions, narcissism and cruelty toward their fellow man?

Social media has created an audience that lives online instead of in the moment. You see parents at the school play ignoring the live event because they're buried in their phones trying to upload the photo they just took. You see people holding up their phones to record others who have fallen or humiliated themselves in some way. Helping the afflicted never enters their minds because they're too busy being the first to exploit the humiliation and therefore, be more "social."

We have all seen the social media savvy couple sharing a restaurant meal, and both have their heads buried in a phone. They ignore each other so they can be more "social." So there I am watching in amazement as they share cat videos or feverishly express their outrage over someone's comment that claimed their previous post was outrageous. They pause to complain out loud about the restaurant's poor Wi-Fi service which sends them back to their phones to post their outrage all over the restaurant's social media outlets.

The word "outrage" takes a beating in social media. Whether angry or happy, most contributors appear ready to explode at any moment. How are these people alive at the end of the day? You would think spontaneous combustion would have occurred by now.

Users tout the purity of social media communication yet so many contributors hide behind anonymous personas. Users, whose identities are known, earn suspensions or lose jobs because they mistakenly believe the so-called purity of the system justifies any selfish rant.

Social media can be constructive. I'm not denying that there are some wonderful examples out there where it has helped those in need. I think dads shy away from it because we don't want to sift through all the outrage to unearth the good stuff. Why go looking for a fight when we already have enough confrontation in our lives?

One final note - Personally, I avoid social media because I know myself too well. My argumentative DNA would turn hours into days, and days into months. Before long, I'd have the Howard Hughes fingernails, and my hair/beard combo would be declared a wildlife refuge.

SOAP OPERA SPORTS COVERAGE

As a young sports fan in the early '80s, the cable television explosion changed my world. In addition to my local teams, I could watch highlights of any team through the magic of cable sports programming. Back then you saw detailed highlights of every game, and the focus remained on the games. That lasted for about a decade, and it was sports bliss. I could turn on the TV and catch up on everything I'd missed the day before.

Fast-forward to today. We have more sports coverage than ever before so everything should be better. Strangely, it's not.

Go ahead. Tune into your favorite sports network and see how long you have to wait before a story about what's happening on the field enters the rotation. If your screen is large enough, you can read the scores scrolling across the bottom but highlights are in short supply. Once the highlights arrive, you see maybe three or four plays from each game even though there are more people covering the event than ever before.

How did we get to this point? Today's networks value commentary over pure sports coverage. At some point, they decided sports fans were more interested in off-the-field stories. That memo didn't come from dads. We just want sports, but the networks insist we want something else.

So now whenever an athlete does something blatantly wrong, the networks run an endless rotation of talking heads to enlighten those of us who are apparently incapable of determining right from wrong.

The enlightenment doesn't end there. Now we must endure more talking heads as they pontificate on suspected or perceived wrongs that athletes may or may not have committed. Hours of programming are dedicated to teams of "insiders" who often strive to create drama where no drama should exist.

When I turn on the TV today to find out what happened on the field, I have to sit through segment after segment of painfully obvious commentary. If you're lucky enough to stumble across highlights, you only see plays that end in home runs, touchdowns, dunks and goals. There was a day when sports programming would offer detailed breakdowns of critical drives or rallies, but those don't exist anymore. Today they give more air time to a player's signature touchdown dance than they do to the critical drive that made the dance possible.

Network executives used to point to their ratings to justify their soap opera programming. That's because men will choose poor sports programming over most anything else. We all know bad guys should be punished, but we fans watch sports to get away from life's trials and tribulations. After a while, you grow weary of the noise and satisfy your sports fix online. That exodus is reflected in the ever-shrinking ratings of certain networks, and the aforementioned network executives are left scratching their heads.

Some of the sports programming is borderline comedy. How many panel members are necessary for a football program? There are so many "experts" providing commentary that each person only has about five seconds to speak during each segment. And thank goodness they do, so we fans can benefit from insightful comments such as, "Someone needs to step up."

One final note - Could anything be more annoying than

interviewing coaches during games? The exchanges are always uncomfortable. Just once, I wish a coach would answer from the heart during a sideline interview.

Reporter: "Coach, what are you going to tell your team during halftime?

Coach: "I'll tell them as bad as we played in this first half, it could be worse. We could be empty-headed sideline reporters trolling for nonexistent drama."

Reporter: "Coach was the suspension of John Smith a distraction for your team?"

Coach: "Not at all. I suppose if he were a starter, then maybe a little. But you're talking about our third-string cornerback. I didn't even know his name until you mentioned it."

Reporter: "What a great victory. How do you feel right now?"

Coach: "I feel very lucky. Our quarterback had a dead body in his trunk yesterday but no one is pressing charges (wink, wink). And I feel extremely blessed that none of our linemen have tested positive for God only knows what they're taking."

WHERE IS THE OUTRAGE OVER THE DAD STEREOTYPE?

There is no shortage of lively articles and commentary regarding the objectification of women in commercials, movies and TV shows - and justifiably so. I don't know anyone who would disagree with that premise. However, women are not the only victims of such profiling injustice. Where is the outrage over the portrayal of dads by these same institutions?

If you recently landed on Earth and tried to understand our culture by watching television, you would believe dads are just below pencils on an evolutionary scale. These portrayals classify most dads as moronic knuckle draggers who would walk off a cliff if left alone. Other portrayals include the greedy business dad, the aloof dad and the ever-popular absent dad. While those dads certainly exist, you are led to believe that competent, engaged fathers don't exist.

I have a running joke with my kids about how most children-oriented movies kill off the dad either during or before the storyline. Run through your catalogue of kid's movies and tell me I'm wrong. There are a few exceptions, but the general trend is clear.

The entertainment industry promotes the notion that dads

are not only incapable of taking care of themselves; they are incapable of taking care of their own children. The notion is woefully outdated yet no one seems to care. In fact, I see many women on television nod their heads in agreement when tired notion rears its ugly head.

I run into these women all the time in my every-day life and I've always found it odd that they wear this misguided belief like a badge of honor. They come out of the woodwork when they find out my wife is traveling somewhere alone. They come right up to me and tell me how awesome my wife is and I agree whole heartedly. Unfortunately, it doesn't end there. Instead, it morphs into a lecture on how it's about time she is getting away for a few days. And their tone suggests that her need to get away would never occur to me.

Then they ask me what I'm going to do while she's gone with a smirk that says, "It's your turn to suffer now baby!" Others ask the same question out of genuine concern. Once I replied to one of these worried moms that the kids and I had plenty of cigarettes and jerky to get by. I said if we run out of jerky, we could set some traps for the raccoons by the trash cans. She wouldn't let her kid come over to play while my wife was gone, and she dropped off some food on day two. You could tell she desperately wanted to come in and check on the kids. I was going to ask her how to light the microwave, but I was afraid she'd call the authorities.

My wife is an amazing woman. She accomplishes more in a day than most people do in a week. Her patience is legendary, and she is a wonderful role model for our children. That said, my wife's job is in the evening while I work during the day. The kids are in school during the day nine months out of the year so do the math. I spend more time alone with my six children than she does. My wife understands this but somehow this fact escapes the other moms. Amazingly, my children haven't burned down the house, missed an appointment or starved under my care. Somehow the laundry gets done, and the kitchen is usually clean when my wife returns. And any theory that I am aided by aliens or elves is dispelled by the fact that my teenagers' shoes sit near the front door. Trust me; the odor emanating from those shoes would chase away or incapacitate most life forms.

There was a time when dads never changed a diaper or washed the dishes. I know because my dad was one of them, and he readily admitted it. That world hasn't existed in decades. Some dads are more involved than others, and every situation is different. Sure, dads come home from the grocery store with more junk food, and we may take the kids on burger runs when faced with day three of leftovers, but we are engaged and have been for some time.

So hear me objectified women, and your outraged supporters, we dads join you in your struggle as one of the entertainment world's worst cases of mistaken identity.

That said, I'd like to share a little honesty on the whole objectification thing from a dad's point of view. Dads have a different and more self-serving view of objectification on the rare occasion it's aimed at us.

Any dad my age would be flattered at being objectified by anyone, any time. It doesn't mean we're open for business but the fact that a member of the opposite sex would give us a second look provides a huge morale boost. At this point in my life, there are only two reasons a female would approach a dad like me. She is either orchestrating a fundraiser or wants me to help put chairs away after an event.

One final note – During a business trip to Las Vegas, I entered an elevator alone and a lady in a black dress scurried inside as the doors were closing. When she said her floor, something seemed off to me. Then she asked me, and I quote, "Where is handsome man like you headed tonight?" At that point I realized she was actually a "he" and while both of us laughed off the comment, I still count that as a victory. I have to because they're so rare.

GOTCHA

I have been a news junky for most of my adult life. My first job was a reporter, and it's still in my blood. I've endured more city council and board of education meetings than I care to remember. Back then my news directors wouldn't let me run with a story unless I had confirmed sources. This was before news morphed into entertainment.

Fast-forward to today. News outlets run stories based on rumor, and reporters are under pressure to be first instead of correct. They trip over each other to post a story like kids chasing after parade candy. Sadly, individuals and entities have their names dragged through the mud without proof or confirmation.

What really scares me is the "gotcha" nature of today's coverage.

Some people say truly awful things that deserve ridicule or punishment. The instances that bother me involve well-intentioned people who say or do something regrettable. The news outlets will focus only on the mistake and ignore anything positive the latest victim has accomplished. The mistake is replayed countless times and examined as if it were some rare archeological find. This coverage threatens careers and thrives on humiliation. Then the lazy media will start overanalyzing the mistake to milk a few more days out of the story. They'll drop it as soon as the next mistake occurs.

News flash to the "gotcha" vultures: All of us make mistakes. I've made more than my share but thankfully a television crew wasn't following me around.

If a camera crew recorded the private conversations any of us have had with our siblings and closest friends, we would all be under siege.

And I love it when media members make inflammatory statements about someone else's so-called inflammatory statement. They build a verbal bonfire to stir up the masses but the general public yawns as we dare to believe the sun will rise the next day even though we disagree with the media. Then the angle quickly changes to media outrage (there's that word again) over the fact that no one else thinks the inflammatory statement is inflammatory.

Today's news outlets crank out more opinion than news. A current television news segment involves one story followed by everyone's reaction. Then you have reactions to the reactions. Then the more inflammatory reactions become their own stories thus the gotcha approach feeds the news cycle without the nuisance of legitimate news gathering.

One final note – The media shouldn't be allowed to use the popular "sources say" reference without identifying the source. If they don't identify the source, they should have to say "This just in from my imagination..." or "According to my invisible friend Mr. Fiction..."

WHEN DID ATTITUDE REPLACE COMPOSURE AS A DESIRED ATTRIBUTE?

If you're a dad with daughters, you are exposed to copious amounts of television programming aimed at preadolescent females. It's usually noise in the background. However, when you have daughters watching, the alarming portrayals of preadolescent TV characters quickly capture a dad's attention. These portrayals deliver a steady diet of female characters with "attitude." In such cases, attitude is a code word for rude, selfish behavior. And this behavior is praised and rewarded as these mini divas get everything they want despite their poor behavior.

As a dad, I wonder who keeps coming up with these characters? The TV tweens dress like provocative adults and treat their TV parents like pond scum. Only a given show's laugh track thinks this is funny. You could advise your daughter to avoid a particular program but these portrayals are ubiquitous.

You might think I'm overreacting but kids are self-centered enough as it is. And the girls can be particularly cruel to each other. They don't need coaching on how to be a better bitch. Are there any dads on the production staffs of these shows raising their hands and asking, "What the hell are we doing here?"

Why does Hollywood insist on portraying selfishness as a strength and selflessness as a weakness?

Look at the adult women on most reality TV shows. A selfish attitude trumps composure most of the time. The more outrageous the behavior, the more attention one receives. Then one day you turn around and wonder how the Kardashians became famous. Then a chill runs down your spine when you realize nude selfies and wealth have replaced talent and self-respect.

My brother and I were taking a bus tour of New York City a few years ago. The tour stopped at many historical sites but the passengers rarely left the bus because it was a hot day in June. Then the bus stopped nearby the DASH store (a chain operated by the Kardashians). Women (and one male), who never left the bus for truly historical sites, sprinted from the bus to the DASH store. They returned with several bags and zero dignity. The one male who returned from the store refused to make eye contact with the rest of the men on the bus. He lost his "man card" at the next secret meeting. The dads on the bus exchanged that look that said, "Please don't let that be my daughter one day." My dad brain found the experience disappointing and fascinating at the same time.

One final note – How did we get to the point where obnoxious behavior (fictional and non-fictional) may run unabated under the guise of empowerment. And the self-appointed self-esteem police keep careful watch how we respond. So when someone is being rude to me, I must navigate the politically correct waters by referring to said person as empowered. If this person insults me, I am required to praise said person's confidence. Our shaming culture prevents me from referring to rude behavior as… you know, rude.

TV TRAUMA (ARE YOU A VICTIM?)

The increasing number of retro television channels has me suffering from something I like to call *TV Trauma*. As a child raised in the television era, my scars run deep.

TV Trauma occurs when you come across a show you loved as a child only now you watch the program through an adult's eyes. You stare at the screen in horror wondering what you ever saw in the program. The truly sad part is you still remember each episode - just like your kids recognize every *SpongeBob Squarepants* episode within the first five seconds.

TV Trauma is especially rampant among those of us who grew up in the '70s and early '80s.

For instance, watch an episode of *Welcome Back Kotter* now, and you'll lose faith in humanity. You'll shake your head in disbelief wondering why you sprinted home to watch as a child. When you hear people laugh at the signature phrase, "Up your nose with a rubber hose," you suddenly understand why parents of that era thought everyone younger than them was on drugs.

Can you imagine someone pitching shows like *Sanford & Son*, *Good Times* and The *Jeffersons* in today's politically correct climate? Today's PC watch dogs would suffer conniption fits if something like *All in the Family* hit the air today.

The lock, stock and barrel formula shows like *Fantasy Island* and *Love Boat* look silly by today's standards. The plots are more repetitive than campaign promises, but I remember watching them with great anticipation. When I hear people say, "…jump the shark," a chill runs up my spine because I actually tuned in to watch Fonzi jump the shark! And I cared!

Some of the vintage science fiction shows haven't aged well. I'll give some shows a pass on special effects because they were limited by the technology of their time. That said, some programs stumbled badly out of the gate and father time has only exacerbated the situation.

Reruns of the late '70s Buck Rodgers TV show are flat out painful to watch. The show's comedy relief robot (named Twiki and voiced by legendary artist Mel Blanc) sounds like a hung-over Porky Pig speaking through a box fan. And the space battles repeatedly featured the same handful of stock shots.

Some of the trauma occurred immediately. The live-action Spiderman TV series of the late '70s nearly ruined my childhood. During the show's short run, even a comic book fan boy like me had trouble swallowing the show's poor production values. You could practically see the stage hand (off camera) throwing the piece of rope that was supposed to be Spiderman's signature webbing. It was as if the network gave the producers a script, $400 for production and a good-luck slap on the back. Today I could create more convincing special effects using whatever is available in my garage.

Some of the shows from that era still hold up such as *Rockford Files*, *Taxi* and *WKRP*. Unfortunately, for every Jim Rockford there was a "Sit on it Potsie" or "What you talkin' bout Willis" to remind us how low the bar was set for acceptable entertainment.

Don't forget the commercials. A healthy dose of uncomfortableness awaits if you go online and watch some vintage commercials. The themes are so out of touch by today's standards, it's hard to imagine these commercials aired on network television. No one wears seatbelts in cars and moms are pushing Twinkies as wholesome snacks.

I highly recommend watching the cringe-worthy late 1960s muscle car commercials. The attempts to mesh the American auto maker machismo with the flower power culture provide an endless stream of comedic gold. Awkwardness abounds as button-down corporate giants rework the lyrics of the era's most iconic songs into the cheesiest of jingles. If you've never seen these commercials, imagine Disney trying to remake a Quentin Tarantino movie.

The days of three networks are long gone, but I still think today's youth will have their own horror stories. My theory is they'll look back at the current reality TV boom much the same way my generation recalls and denies participation in the disco era. Hey, deny all you want but someone purchased all those *Saturday Night Fever* soundtracks. And for the record, I wanted to learn how to dance like John Travolta but I couldn't afford Deney Terrio's "as seen on TV" instruction guide. I also watched enough episodes of *Soul Train* to know there was no hope for me.

One final note – How many mistakes would you have allowed Gilligan before offering him up to the headhunters? As a young child, I had about eight episodes worth of patience before I came to the conclusion that Gilligan needed to sleep with the fishes.

BEWARE THE HELICOPTER PARENTS AND TREAT MONITORS

As a child playing little league baseball and football in the searing Midwest heat, I don't recall teammates collapsing in droves due to dehydration or exhaustion. Today, kids arrive to practice or games with nine gallons of liquid, and they must hydrate every three minutes or for every five steps they take. Some kids are accompanied by the hovering plastic bubble parents who are there to make sure nothing "bad" happens to their child. And by "bad" I mean, challenging or character-building. I am all for keeping kids safe and healthy but most of us dads cringe at the "wussification" of today's youth.

One morning I was coaching a grade-school boys basketball game. After two trips up and down the court, one of my players called time out on his own. When I asked why, he said he was dehydrated from too much running. We weren't even one minute into the game. Needless to say, Captain Hydration spent some quality time on the bench that day. This was after his mother rushed over with water as if she were tending to a shipwreck survivor who had just washed ashore.

While coaching a grade-school baseball game I watched one of my players hit a single and run to first base. While shouting words of encouragement to the next batter, I saw something out of the corner of my eye, and it was moving quickly from the bleachers to the field. As I looked closer, I realized it was a mother running to first base to give her son a drink of water because he had run 60 feet. Do these families keep bottles of water by the front door for anyone who may have to make that death-defying walk to the mailbox or a parked car?

And when did socially acceptable snacks become a cult-like experience? When I was young, we would have the occasional cooler of soda or ice cream after the game, but it was never expected. Today there is more attention on the post-game snack schedule than anything else. Why focus on the valuable lessons sports offer when there are more important things like making sure kids are eating gluten free, sugar free, high fructose corn syrup free snacks wrapped in recycled unisex packaging?

These treat monitors fret about the health of today's youth yet the first thing they do when they see a kid exercise for ten seconds is throw food at them. Kids are resilient if you give them a chance, but they also know how to milk a hyper-sensitive parent for all the snacks they can get. And these parents are mystified that their child is in poor physical condition even though said child has been playing sports all year round.

And don't get me started on the "everyone makes the team" mentality because that has its own chapter later.

One final note – Just once I would love to bring a carton of cigarettes and a funnel cake on my designated treat day just to watch the treat monitors pass out.

IS EVERYONE A VICTIM NOW?

There are true victims out there who need help but the word "victim" seemingly applies to everyone now. Over the last few years, my fatherly BS meter has detected more "manufactured victims" than ever before. The common denominator of these manufactured victims is they assume zero accountability for poor decisions.

I remember the first time I heard a commercial asking me if I suffered from Credit Card Debt Disorder. The commercial made it sound as if these CCDD victims woke up one day and boom, they were in debt up to their eyeballs through no fault of their own. Of course the commercials put all the blame on the credit card issuers. Do they have CCDD support group meetings? I'd love to hear some of the quotes from those support meetings...

> "I walked into my living room and there was a 60 inch TV and a commercial grade sound system! I stepped over two tablets, three smart phones and a neglected collection notice to get a better look. After binge watching three series on Netflix and ordering a round of drinks at the bar later that night, I realized the credit card companies were taking advantage of me. That's when I knew I was a CCDD victim."

While there are shopaholics who need help, this commercial was taking it to the absurd by suggesting that anyone over a certain amount of debt is a victim. Sure some credit card issuers may take advantage of the novice user but the user has no responsibility here? Look, we all say, do, purchase and eat things we know are detrimental to our budget and health. Most of us know the fault rests squarely on our shoulders but each day we create more excuses and accountability keeps fading.

I carry extra weight around my midsection. I know it's because of my diet. I exercise but I like to eat too many fattening foods to have a chiseled torso. Today I see commercial after commercial telling me that my inability to lose weight is not my fault. Funny how most of the solutions involve purchasing the one program or pill that will cure all. The solution is rarely more exercise and sensible eating. Instead it's a short cut for poor victims, like me, who choose biscuits and gravy over lettuce... er um... I mean I had biscuits and gravy forced down my throat by the evil companies that make it and/or distribute it.

I have a large family so we don't eat out often because it's too expensive. We eat fairly healthy because my wife is very good at making sure we eat a balanced diet. If I were in charge of the menu, it would frighten every nutritionist on the planet. I love to eat what I eat and I take responsibility for my actions. I'm not going to hop aboard the excuse train to feel better about myself.

I've watched other families eat out often and they pack on the pounds as a result. I have no problem with that until the parents of those families come marching into schools to complain that the lunch program is fattening up their children. Or they blame a fast food chain for serving them fattening food. That would be the same food these "victims" ordered and ate of their own free will.

The victim logic is tantalizing because it's easy to put accountability on a shelf. Why go for a walk and watch my carb intake when I can sue a giant fast food chain?

One final note – It won't be long before someone reaches the ultimate zero accountability mode when he or she wakes up with a hangover and doesn't recognize the person in bed next to them. This "victim" will file three lawsuits. The first one will be against the auto company for selling the car that transported the victim to and from the bar; next is the bar for providing a venue in which to drink and meet strangers; and finally the beer company for making it all seem like a good idea after about eight beers into the evening.

ARE MAGNET SCHOOLS AFFECTING EARTH'S ORBIT?

When you're the father of six children, you get an up-close view of several schools. I've watched schools try to differentiate themselves by branding themselves as a "magnet" or "blue ribbon" institution. There are other designations, but those are the most common I've experienced. The problem is once that arms race begins, you start seeing those titles on all schools so once again, they all appear the same.

Where do they go from there? Are they going to keep inventing new titles in order to differentiate? Will we start seeing "Electromagnet" schools? If I donate laptops to one of these schools will the hard drives be erased once they enter the building? Will schools start vying for multiple ribbon colors? And what is the color hierarchy? Will a red ribbon school be better than a blue ribbon school? The schools don't seem to be doing anything different from each other, but business is booming with bumper sticker vendors.

Colleges and universities play this differentiation game through an ever-expanding list of rankings. What started as a handful of rankings a few decades ago has exploded into its own industry. Today there are rankings for every aspect of the college experience and just about every school can claim to be in the top five of at least one ranking.

So if you're looking for a college that offers the most affordable business degree on a campus with the nation's most extreme rock-climbing wall, and a food service that offers the most amazing apple turnovers on Tuesdays, I'm sure there is a ranking for that.

One final note – If math or science-based magnet schools had been around when I was in school, I would have been physically unable to attend. The building would have repelled me as a "like" magnetic pole - based on my weakness in math and science. I would have ended up in a nonstick surface school where the students slip and slide down the hallways to avoid mathematical word problems.

PARENT FASHION

Once women and men become parents, fashion is quickly replaced by whatever is comfortable and available. Parents of newborns gladly trade time spent on conscious fashion decisions for a few extra minutes of sleep. Comfort trumps everything else. While moms do a much better job in their attempts to look presentable in public, dads seem to care less about their wardrobe and general appearance with each passing year.

Like many parents of infants, I've gone to work not realizing there is a waterfall of baby formula barf running down the back of my shirt. Yes, there are towels that help mitigate the infant's assault on your shoulder but my babies would easily navigate that barrier with surgical precision. And when someone at work finally points out the mess, we dads just shrug it off and move on while our shirt resembles a paper mache project gone horribly wrong. It's not like we want the crusty waterfall on our shirt, we're just too tired or too busy to care.

Parents who attempt to wear spandex should know their limits. If fitting into your pants requires two people to hold your pants open while you jump off your roof into them, you probably shouldn't be wearing those pants. As my wife once said, spandex-oriented clothing should come in "ages" instead of "sizes." The tags should read, "You must be between the ages of 18 – 25 to wear this item." A warning on the label should read, "Caution: Just because you can squeeze into these, doesn't mean you should."

Some moms try to dress like their daughters. Please stop. It's not a question of whether you can physically pull it off because many of you can. Let your daughters have their own fashion trends. There are age appropriate fashions for all of you and you'll look great in whatever you wear (that's my husband training kicking in). Otherwise, you look more desperate than the hipster dads. Okay, I take that back. Nothing screams desperation like hipster dads.

One final note – I've made many late-night medicine runs for ailing kids. One winter night I left the house at 2 a.m. which meant I dressed in the dark and grabbed whatever was by the door. As a result, I walked into the store wearing boots that didn't match and my sweat pants were inside out and backward. My daughter's pink hat rested crookedly on my head and my sweatshirt looked like I had recently emerged from a paint factory explosion. That night I ran into an ex-girlfriend I hadn't seen in years. The look on her face said it all so I vocalized what I knew she was thinking. I posed like a catalog model and said, "Obviously, you dodged a bullet."

TIRED YOUNG PEOPLE

All parents have experienced this. You spent the night caring for an infant who woke up every couple of hours and one of the older kids who threw up in bed, twice. By some miracle, you arrive to work on time the next morning ready to get something done. You're already thirty minutes into your day and in walks the young coworker who complains how tired they are because they were out late with friends or binge watching their new, favorite show. They behave as if the act of showing up for work is on par with landing on the moon and the rest of the free world should acknowledge their greatness.

Before I go any further, I need to take a few steps back and admit something. Before my "married with children" days, I remember coming home from work and taking a nap for as long as I wanted. I remember wondering why my older coworkers were always cranky or resembled the undead. My mindset back then seems hilarious to me now. So while I want to laugh in the young, tired person's face and explain the true definition of tired, I have to remind myself that I was once the young, tired person.

What troubles me is a new breed of young, tired people who harbor a sense of entitlement quite foreign to my generation. Picture me standing on my front lawn wearing sandals and black socks as I elaborate.

Today I let the young, tired person's rant go and hope said person will settle down and get on with the workday. Some do. Unfortunately, others shift the whining gears to the entitlement rant. You know… the rant where no one appreciates their work or their incredible ideas. They believe everything that comes out of their head is pure gold, and they bristle at the mere hint that someone may question this undeniable fact. They become upset if their greatness isn't acknowledged every fifteen minutes yet they are quick to mock others with more life and work experience. These are the nomads who frequently change jobs because no one truly understands their greatness.

Ten years from now, these same people will be rolling their eyes at the next generation of young, tired people. The circle of life continues.

One final note – I'll never forget the time when a young, tired person marched into my office and expressed outrage at not having reached a director level position after a whopping six months on the job. Assuming this person was kidding, I upped the ante to vice president and the response was shockingly serious. This person graciously admitted a VP position was probably too much to expect after only six months on the job. However, the director level position was apparently long overdue. I had to subdue my initial response (which was uncontrollable laughter) and spent a good thirty minutes convincing this poor soul not to leap off the ledge of disenfranchisement.

WHEN DID COMPETITION BECOME A BAD THING?

Most dads cringe at participation trophies. It's not some overly macho man code of honor. Men and women who grew up playing competitive sports, before the dawn of the self-esteem movement, find the concept of "everyone makes the team" perplexing.

The "everyone makes the team and plays" concept is fine for kids younger than say 10 or 11, but this chapter focuses on youth sports involving kids between that age and high school.

Today the self-esteem police and their loyal followers like to shame dads into the notion that if a kid fails to make an athletic team; the kid's life will spiral into a gorge of failure and sadness. Dads (and moms), who have played sports, roll their eyes at this logic because we know where this leads. It doesn't lead to a kinder, gentler existence. It leads to unprecedented apathy fostered by a total lack of competition.

When I didn't make an athletic team as a child, it was a punch to the gut but it also forced me to work harder and improve if I truly wanted to play. And shockingly, if I still couldn't make the team with my best effort, I was able to move on with my life without a grief counselor and life coach. Back then there was only one school team and the coaches had to make (gasp!) cuts. And if the child was upset about not making the team, the parents sided with the coach (gasp again!) and trusted his/her judgement.

Today's kids have zero incentive to improve because they know they will be handed a spot on any of their school's two or three teams. All they have to do is show up. As a result, we have too many teams and not enough courts or fields to house the ever-expanding number of games. Parents and coaches are forced to drive around in pattern resembling Daffy Duck's directions to Planet X just to find a place to play.

The self-esteem police are blind to an important element of childhood competition. The kids who want to be coached and want to improve are cheated by the kids who don't care enough to improve or are just there because their parents want them out of the house. The kids who don't care about improving disrupt the learning process for everyone else. They interrupt the flow of practices and live competition with their "I'm bored" antics or lazy approach. This ultimately penalizes the kids who truly want to work hard and improve.

If you have coached young kids, you know exactly what I'm talking about. If these disruptive kids didn't make the cut, maybe they would appreciate the opportunity a little more the next time and make more of an effort to improve. Instead, we are teaching our kids that they will make any team they want without ever lifting a finger to improve themselves.

This is why we have so many club or select teams. The day we adopted the "everyone makes the team and plays" philosophy, we opened the flood gates to the club/select team approach. It had to be done so the truly competitive kids had an opportunity to develop and, in theory, have more fun.

Today's world of select teams can get a little crazy. Some of these teams travel more than an NBA star on his way to the basket during the playoffs. And don't forget the crazed parents who are convinced their child is destined for a professional career due to a strict training regimen of texting, video gaming and lying down.

One final note – During my time as a youth sports coach, my favorite "everyone plays" moment was when one of my players chased a basketball that had rolled out of bounds and into a lobby. The kid disappeared through the door and we all waited for him to return. After an uncomfortably long period of time, I hustled to the lobby to make sure my player didn't fall and hurt himself. Luckily I found him perfectly healthy with the ball under his arm. Unfortunately, he was standing in the concession line because his stomach was growling. I rest my case.

Jim Maxwell

DADS AND VOLUNTEERING

Parents willingly or unwillingly volunteer for a variety of services usually associated with schools and churches. The schools (especially the private schools) expect a certain level of volunteering and rightfully so. Moms and dads answer the bell but their approach to volunteer work differs greatly.

Moms treat volunteer work like a social event. They view it as a way to connect with friends and enjoy the camaraderie.

Dads typically show up to do their time and move on. There is the rare dad who networks the room but most of us are there to put in our time and go home. We are pleasant enough and happy to help but we're not there to make new friends and gossip. It's just not how most of us are wired.

Volunteering is a riskier proposition for dads because often the dad who shows up ends up being one of the few males in attendance. You feel like a rogue animal that wandered into an unfamiliar herd on the Serengeti. Members of the herd avoid you like the plague. Conversations grind to a halt as you approach. When you try to make small talk you are rewarded with looks of confusion and panic.

I've also learned a golden rule which bears repeating to any new dads out there. Never (I repeat, NEVER) try to suggest changes to an event that has been run by the same crew of women for several years. The longer a particular group of women have been in charge of a specific event, the more resistant they are to suggestions.

Don't get me wrong. These women are the life blood of churches, schools and parishes and they should be commended for their service. However, try to suggest a more efficient way to do something and I promise you that won't end well. Their demeanor immediately changes from angel to Bond villain. If you were standing on a trap door that led to a shark tank, they'd drop you through the door and go right back to brewing more coffee.

One final note – Once I was cleaning tables at a fundraising event run by a group of dads whose daughters attended the same school. It was a rare occasion where all the volunteers were dads. While I scrubbed away at the table tops, a woman approached me with a look on her face that made me think, "Oh no, did I do something wrong?" She pointed out that a female had entered the kitchen area to help some of the dads locate supplies. She gleefully pronounced that the men couldn't seem to get through one event without the help of a woman. I tried to deflect the awkwardness of the moment by saying, "If you had a bunch of men using your kitchen, wouldn't you want to come in and check on them once in a while?"

I resumed my cleaning and assumed she would go away but she didn't. She kept going about how the hapless dads needed a woman to bail them out. After enduring a few more jabs, I pointed to the kitchen and said, "You mean that lady with the green dress? Actually, that's my brother so technically I think we're okay. Sometimes he just likes to dress up when he goes out and thank goodness for us he really knows his way around a kitchen." Her retreat was swift and satisfying. The person in the kitchen wasn't my brother but I was desperate to end the conversation before I said something I would regret.

THE EXTENDED ISOLATION PRINCIPLE

It's amazing how quickly dads regress to their pre-husbandly way of life when left alone for a few days. And by alone, I mean no wife and no kids. If dads are left alone for one day or mom leaves the kids behind, the transformation does not occur. If dads are left completely alone for a period of time that exceeds 24 hours, the transformation is quick and strikingly thorough.

On the few occasions my wife and kids have been gone for an extended period of time, my transformation has been miraculous. Cereal for every meal becomes reasonable again. Clothes and shaving become optional. If you do wear something, it's not coming off for days.

Household priorities are reversed. The isolated dad falls behind on washing dishes and laundry. However, he catches up on where his old albums were hiding and whatever Netflix series was on his binge list.

Additional sleep allows the isolated dad to remain awake and alert much later than usual. He interrupts the household's usual parade of cartoons and reality shows by reuniting with news and sports programming. Isolated dad will watch the same sports highlights or news footage over and over just because he can!

Existence is true bliss as years of husbandly programming gives way to baser instincts.

Time is abundant, and the almighty schedule is suddenly rendered irrelevant. If not for his job keeping him on some sort of schedule, the isolated dad would stagger up to a sports bar at 4 a.m. wondering why the place wasn't open for lunch.

It all comes to a screeching halt when isolated dad suddenly freezes in mid stride when he glances at his watch on the day of his family's return. This sobering slap in the face never seems to surface until just a few hours before the missing household members are scheduled to return. The isolated cave dad is momentarily paralyzed as he takes inventory of his neglectful ways. The fear grows as he examines each room and frantically hatches a plan to remedy the situation before the appearance of his soon to be angry wife.

His survival instinct kicks in and he becomes a whirlwind of house-keeping activity. The speed at which his disaster recovery plan moves is a thing of beauty. Incidentally, this highly efficient performance is like the Sasquatch legend of husbandry. It's never displayed in front of his spouse for fear of additional cleaning assignments. Wives may suspect it exists but they've never witnessed it in real time. Wives and children who lay claim to eye witness accounts are dismissed as crazy or desperate for attention. Cynics point to the lack of photographic evidence to support these accounts. And the few photos that do exist are suspect and therefore, inconclusive.

Once the family arrives, isolated dad believes he has executed a seamless recovery. Never mind that during his cleaning frenzy he may have left a dozen clues that even the Warren Commission couldn't miss.

One final note - If my wife and kids left me alone for a couple of months, they would return to find me in the middle of the family room naked and buried in a pile of empty pizza boxes and cereal. I'd be listening to a comedy album the kids never knew I owned. My children wouldn't recognize me thanks to my casual approach to hygiene and they would have difficulty understanding me as I could only communicate through a series of grunts (having lost the ability to speak). A few days later, I would return to my fatherly form.

Jim Maxwell

BOX TICKER COUPLES

Dads tend to avoid keeping tabs on which spouse does what and when. Our memories are limited so we save our available memory banks for important things like random pop culture references and where to find the best pizza. Most dads don't keep track of their wives' social calendars because we figure it all evens out down the road. Many wives do the same. Some couples take a much different approach. I call them the box ticker couples.

You rarely see them together, but you'll hear them justifying every excursion outside of their house to anyone within shouting distance.

These are the couples who believe daily life must be partitioned into equal segments and everything must come out even at the end of the week to prevent their fragile marriage from unraveling.

You hear them say things like, "If so and so thinks I am going to watch the kids alone three nights in one week, then so and so can watch them the whole weekend while I'm gone doing whatever."

These people are particularly scary around holidays, birthdays and anniversaries as they proudly outline the consequences their spouse will face if the correct gift doesn't materialize.

They bring their crying infant to the restaurant and the theater because they both deserve a night out. Never mind that they ruin the night for the rest of us who took the time to get a sitter or are flying solo so we could enjoy one night away from our own crying infants.

They treat life as if it's a turn-based game of equality and symmetry. Family life rarely accommodates this approach. Therefore, these people are in a constant state of stress. Unfortunately, they feel compelled to share their perceived victimization with anyone who may appear to be enjoying themselves.

I married a woman who is not a box ticker. In fact, we encourage each other to take advantage of any opportunity that offers either of us a brief escape from parenthood because those opportunities are so rare. If only one of us can escape, the one left behind will gladly help boost the prisoner over the wall before the guards (our children) discover the missing prisoner. And let me be perfectly honest here, if my wife and I kept careful track of our social outings over any period of time, the tiny size of that report would be a sad commentary on our current social lives. We are better off not knowing.

I can't imagine the household of a box ticker couple. Do they hold staff meetings at the kitchen table where they review a master list of who went where and when? Do they bring in a third party quality control specialist to determine the difference between quality time away and actual time away? Do they review a spreadsheet of previous gifts to ensure all are of equal value and status? Do they put the marriage status on high alert if one spouse logged more time out of the house during a given week? Do they install a fingerprint reader by the front door to measure time away?

One final note – Box ticker couples record videos of birthdays just like the rest of us. The difference is they don't do it to remember a family milestone; they plan to submit the recording as evidence during the "gift review" portion of their next weekly staff meeting. And each video includes a detailed briefing of who was in attendance, how long they stayed, what they contributed and what they were wearing. Greeting cards are sent off to have the signatures authenticated.

Jim Maxwell

WELCOME TO JUDGEMART

I know we all have a higher calling at times but when did a quick trip to the store become a guilt-ridden quest for humanitarian perfection?

If you try to read retail packaging to learn more about a product, you have to plow through the ever-increasing sea of chest-pounding content claiming one vendor is more environmentally conscientious than another. I understand that some take that message to heart. However, those of us who must shop, with several kids in tow, don't have time to read about what percentage of a company's packaging is recycled. We are more interested in the expiration date and whether it's on sale.

I feel the rolling eyes of the enlightened crowd as they pity the poor, Neanderthal dad. Let me explain.

I read nutrition labels and I try to eat well but I'm not going to verbally tackle someone for purchasing a product that doesn't meet the expanding definition of political correctness. I'm too busy herding my own cats. And I'd rather get out of the store quickly than spend precious minutes reading about how the chickens were raised or the latest service trip your employees were forced to … er um… voluntold to … er um… you know what I mean.

I realize people make purchasing decisions based on the behaviors and practices of one company versus another. I applaud the companies that "do the right thing" and still turn a profit. I suppose it comes down to how I was raised. I was raised not to pound your chest when you do good works. The purpose is to do the right thing, not morph it into a promotional opportunity. I am glad we are better stewards of our planet but this escalating battle between companies over which entity is the most environmentally friendly has become more of a marketing ploy than a genuine call to do good.

How far will they go with this shaming approach? Will we start seeing people stationed at the end of each isle to critique the contents of our carts? "Excuse me sir? I couldn't help but notice you have brand x cookies in your cart. Did you know the company that makes those cookies allegedly kicks puppies when people aren't looking?"

And don't forget the guilt trip when you've finally made it to the checkout lane. You can't even purchase your "Fair Trade Certified" fruit and your "Rainforest Alliance Certified" coffee without a cashier asking if you would like to donate to yet another cause. I politely decline, and I feel sorry for these poor cashiers who have to do someone else's fundraising for them. What's next? Will the cashier threaten to announce the entire contents of my cart if I don't donate to the cause of the day? "Attention shoppers. Please direct your attention to checkout lane 9 where Mr. Maxwell refuses to donate to the cause. However, he miraculously has enough cash to purchase name brand cereal instead of the store knock off!"

There is a time and a place for fundraising. Most of us give what we can, when we can. We prefer to choose when and where. For many of us, those decisions are personal and not something we want jammed down our throat or sprung on us while we are holding an infant in one hand and thumbing through coupons with the other.

One final note – The day will come when you are sitting in a restroom stall at a big box retail store and someone will come knocking on the stall door. The knocker will slide a collection basket under the door and ask if you would like to donate to those without indoor plumbing.

Jim Maxwell

AN OVERABUNDANCE OF PARENTING EXPERTISE

All potential parents are clueless until they experience parenthood for themselves.

I did what a lot of parenting newcomers do in anticipation of their first child. I read some books and a few articles. I learned what my wife should eat during various stages of her pregnancy, and I read countless theories on how to raise the ideal child. Once you become a parent, you realized that each child is amazingly unique and each book or article must have been written by someone who never actually raised a child.

My favorite books are the ones written by celebrities after they have their first child. They have one toddler and now they are experts in childbirth and parenting. All you need is a personal chef, a team of nannies, a personal trainer and millions of dollars.

My general rule of thumb is if you haven't dealt with teenagers, you might want to keep your parenting advice to yourself. I'll never forget the time a mother of one toddler was in my kitchen when I opened the back door to shout at one of my teenaged sons who was about to put his younger sister in mortal danger. This mom was mortified that I would raise my voice to one of my children and instructed me to approach him in a more nurturing and constructive manner. If you've raised teenage boys, you're probably cracking a smile while picturing that scenario but that poor soul honestly believed she was helping. My first thought was, "Oh you poor thing. The reality train is going to run over you and you'll never see it coming." My second thought was to put her on a bike and push her off our retaining wall (as my son was about to do to his sister) so I could nurture her in a constructive manner on the way to the hospital.

Have you ever noticed that the parents most willing to offer unsolicited advice often have the most ill-behaved children? While they lecture you on maintaining your children's self-esteem, their highly esteemed children are destroying your basement and tormenting your children. They'll pontificate while everyone in the room can clearly hear the lecturer's child shrieking and taking out whole sections of drywall with airborne toys. Those are truly special moments.

My siblings and I were lucky. We had great parents. We never felt physically threatened by them. Sure, we occasionally found ourselves at the wrong end of a spanking or a vigorous jabbing finger to the sternum during a heated lecture. Looking back, we know we deserved whatever came our way. There was accountability, and we knew when we had crossed the line. And I'm not justifying the actions of truly abusive parents. We all know there is a special place in hell for those people.

Back in the day, my generation dreaded the parental backlash when we did something really stupid or destructive. It was an effective deterrent. Today, parents are vilified if they dare to institute punishment when the line of acceptable behavior is crossed. Those of us who grew up in the '60s, '70s and '80s remember the occasional spanking or that firm arm grasp as we were led out of the store. It wasn't abuse. It was a clear message that our behavior was unacceptable and more importantly, we learned from it.

Today the self-esteem police have blurred the lines of effective parenting to the point that all disciplinary actions have been replaced by coddling if one is to survive the ever-watchful eye of political correctness. Most dads roll their eyes at such coddling because we know how boys think. Boys will say or do anything to get out of trouble, and they quickly learn which buttons they need to push to pit the coddlers against the non-coddlers. The girls play the game as well, but their approach is a little more cunning.

One final note - Deflection is also on the increase as "enlightened" parents shift the blame of their child's behavior to anything but the child or themselves. The real crime in all this is we're sending these coddled children into a world for which they are grossly unprepared. It's like throwing Don Knotts into an Ultimate Fighting Championship cage and assuring him that he'll be awesome as you close the cage door and sprint in the opposite direction.

Jim Maxwell

ADVICE FOR NEW DADS REGARDING CHILDBIRTH

Fatherhood is more on-the-job training than anything else. That said, I'd like to offer a few tips to any men out there who are about to become fathers.

Before the baby is born, many new dads like to say, "We are having a baby." I'm not sure where this "we" reference started but trust me; you don't want to say that in front of a woman who has already experienced the birthing process. The only reason new dads get away with this phrase is because their wives haven't gone through labor yet. So let me spare you some backlash and remind you that "you" are having nothing. She is having the baby.

When the big moment arrives, you will be treated like pond scum in the delivery room. You will already feel helpless as you watch your wife endure the unpleasantness of the moment, and you can't do much to ease the suffering. And the nurses will add to that helplessness as they go out of their way to ignore your presence and talk over you as you try to coach your wife through the worst of it. The nurses will demote you to ice chip cup duty because they would rather not have you there in the first place. The event itself is magical and life-changing but the only person in the room who wants you there is your wife. Don't take it personally. It's just the way it is.

If you are even thinking of capturing the birth on video, put that idea out of your mind right now. If you start recording once the real contractions begin, she'll kick you and your recording device through the wall and no one could blame her. And honestly, your friends don't want to come over to your place for dinner and a delivery video. Forget about cameras and just be there for your wife.

As a sign of the times, some women have tried to "Tweet" during labor. My first thought is surely these Twitter-savvy moms must be new to the birthing process. Based on what I've experienced in the delivery room, I imagine the tweets from the mother-to-be would read something like this:

4:10 a.m. Water broke. Hospital bound #excited
4:14 a.m. John so nervous. Love him so much. #blessed
4:35 a.m. Checking in. #cantwait
4:40 a.m. Pain not bad. Refused meds. #bringiton
4:55 a.m. Amazing room. John by my side. #thrilled
5:30 a.m. Nurse says pain about to get real. #nofear
5:35 a.m. Declined meds. #igotthis
5:51 a.m. Taking longer than expected. #gettingtired
5:58 a.m. Contractions getting... wait... OMG
6:53 a.m. Idiots won't let me push. #readytopop
7:15 a.m. John sent pain meds nurse away. #letsrethinkthis
7:17 a.m. Will choke John once within reach. #divorce
7:30 a.m. Meds NOW or someone dies. #bigproblem
7:35 a.m. NEVER having sex again! #castration
7:43 a.m. YAAAAAHHHHHH. #watermelonkeyhole
8:15 a.m. Baby out. John getting neck treated. #relief
8:30 a.m. Baby and Mom healthy. #miracle
8:35 a.m. John reviewing restraining order. #separatebeds

Beware the tar diapers your babies will create during their first couple of days. Parents never used to see these because the hospital personnel used to handle the first few newborn diaper changes. Today parents are charged with those early, post-birth diaper changes and they are unlike anything you've ever seen. The first time I saw one (our second baby) I was no stranger to changing diapers but it nearly floored me. The material resembles your childhood images of the black tar in which dinosaurs were trapped back in the day. Your first thought will be, "What the hell is wrong with my baby?" Don't worry; they go away after two or three changes. And besides, you have much more fun to look forward to over the next few months. The out of the diaper and up-the-back explosions, that always seem to occur immediately after a bath, will make the tar diapers look easy.

You are going to make mistakes but don't worry, you'll learn from them.

You will learn to decipher the "I'm hungry" cry from the "I'd rather play than sleep" cry. It's similar to watching a basketball game and spotting the difference between a legitimate offensive charging foul and the dreaded "flop."

The sooner you accept the fact that babies will defecate during a bath or diaper change, the better off you'll be. They also defecate immediately after you've dressed them in outfits that require twelve layers of straps, snaps and flaps. And by the look in their eyes you would swear they know exactly what they're doing. It may sound disgusting but you'll get used to the routine. In fact, you'll be surprised at what you are willing to touch, wipe and clean after a few months on the job.

You'll take your eyes off the baby for two seconds during a diaper change and hear that soul-crushing thud as the baby rolls off the bed. The baby will be fine but you'll feel like the worst parent on the planet. Fear not as there is a way to purge that self-loathing pit in your stomach. Walk into any discount retailer after 10 p.m. and you will immediately feel better about yourself and your parenting skills.

One final note - You think you know what "tired" feels like, but you don't know "tired" until you've experienced a newborn. When our first baby was keeping us awake, I compared it to having a public address siren inside your house that randomly sounds off until you feed it. Incidentally, you may fall asleep in the chair while feeding the baby but you'll be wide awake on the way back to the baby's room as your foot inevitably lands on the sharpest edge of whatever toy was left on the floor. Oh, and that toy is usually the loudest one in the house which means your infant's eyes will pop wide open just before you reach the crib. Just try not to scream at the young, single coworker who comes up to you the following morning to complain about being tired.

ABOUT THE AUTHOR

Jim grew up in a large family with supportive parents and a close nit group of siblings. The best part of Jim's upbringing was the wicked sense of humor that was allowed to run free in the Maxwell household. That sense of humor provided several "character-building" opportunities throughout Jim's youth, as he slowly discovered his brand of humor was not necessarily embraced by others such as teachers, neighbors and anyone else who had charge of him.

Jim is a professional writer, author and comedian with over 30 years of communications experience. Today, Jim and his wife (Teresa) are the proud parents of six children ages 10 to 22. Discretionary income and uninterrupted thoughts are rarities in the Maxwell household. This is balanced by an abundance of laughter, weirdness, caring, creativity and rows of hot chocolate chip cookies that disappear quickly.

Made in the USA
Lexington, KY
18 September 2016